Anti-Stress
COLOUR BY NUMBERS

Anti-Stress
COLOUR BY NUMBERS

David Woodroffe

ARCTURUS

This edition published in 2021 by Arcturus Publishing Limited
26/27 Bickels Yard, 151–153 Bermondsey Street,
London SE1 3HA

ISBN: 978-1-78950-230-5
CH006909NT
Supplier 29, Date 1120, Print run 10940

Printed in China

Created for children 10+

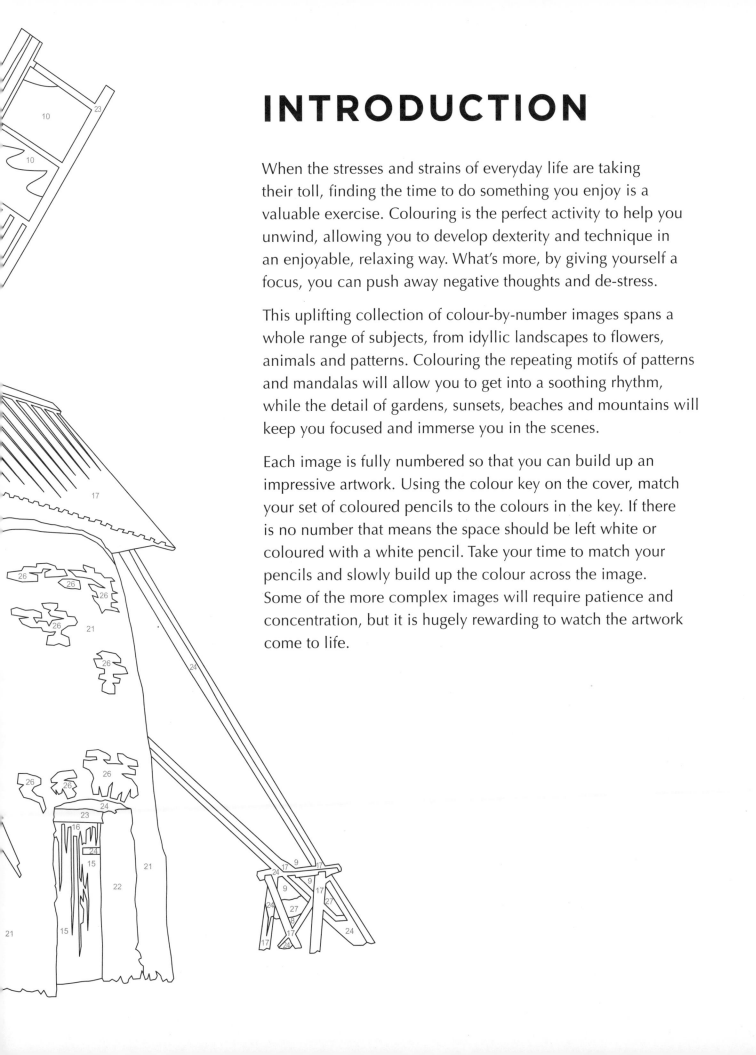

INTRODUCTION

When the stresses and strains of everyday life are taking their toll, finding the time to do something you enjoy is a valuable exercise. Colouring is the perfect activity to help you unwind, allowing you to develop dexterity and technique in an enjoyable, relaxing way. What's more, by giving yourself a focus, you can push away negative thoughts and de-stress.

This uplifting collection of colour-by-number images spans a whole range of subjects, from idyllic landscapes to flowers, animals and patterns. Colouring the repeating motifs of patterns and mandalas will allow you to get into a soothing rhythm, while the detail of gardens, sunsets, beaches and mountains will keep you focused and immerse you in the scenes.

Each image is fully numbered so that you can build up an impressive artwork. Using the colour key on the cover, match your set of coloured pencils to the colours in the key. If there is no number that means the space should be left white or coloured with a white pencil. Take your time to match your pencils and slowly build up the colour across the image. Some of the more complex images will require patience and concentration, but it is hugely rewarding to watch the artwork come to life.

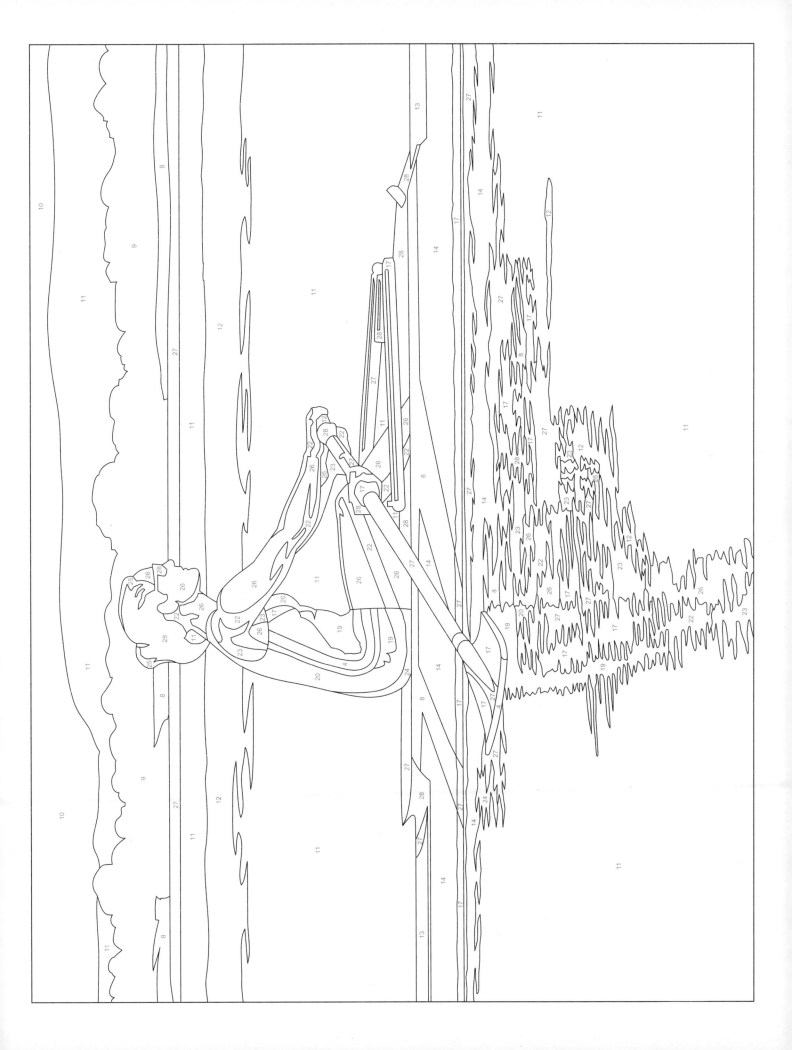

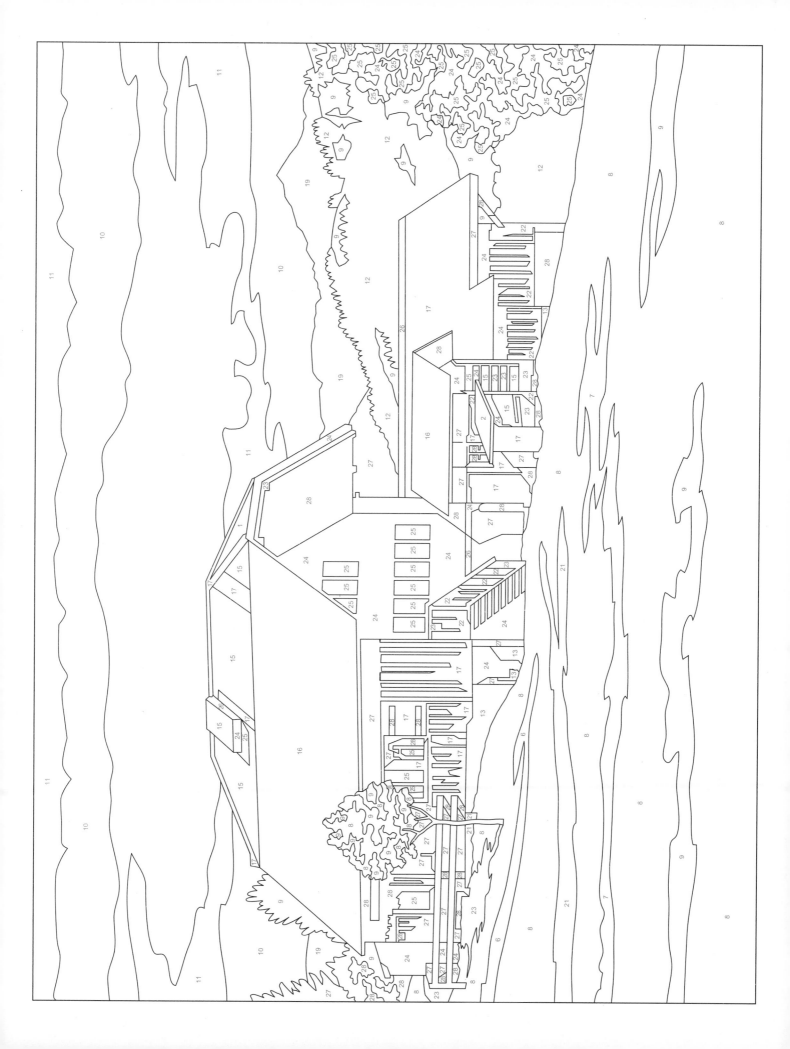

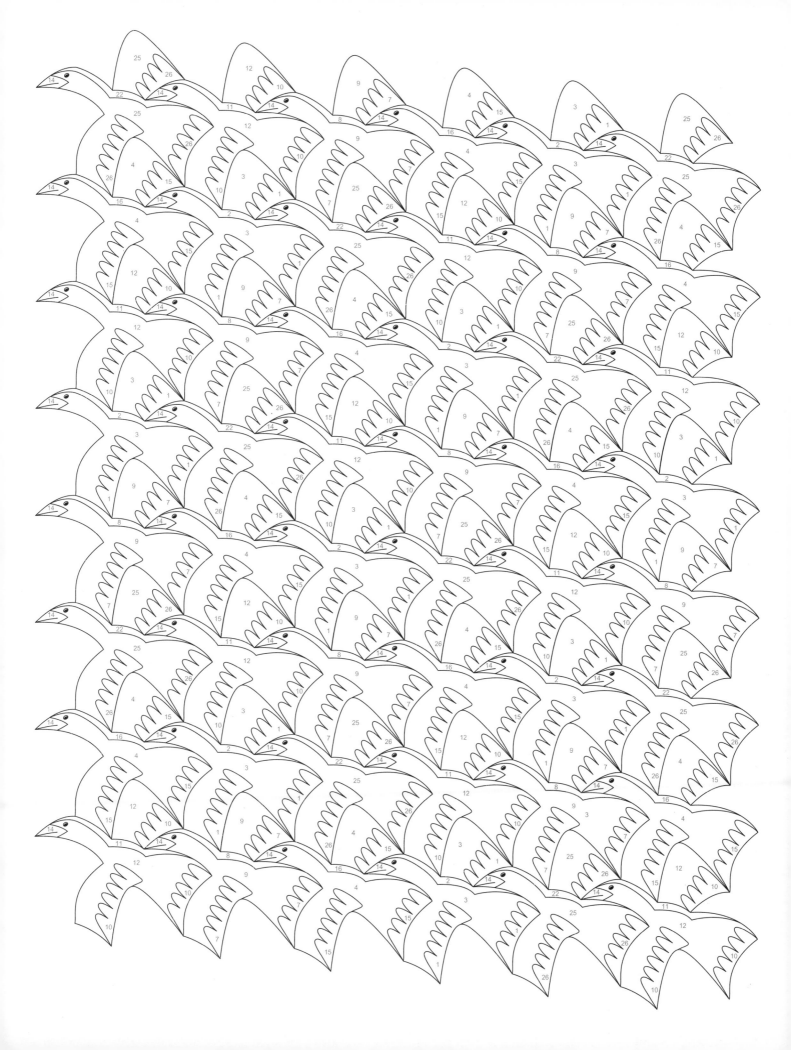